Within My Circle

Ron Benson

Lynn Bryan

Wendy McDonell

Kim Newlove

Charolette Player

Liz Stenson

CONSULTANTS

Harold Fenlon

Ken MacInnis

Elizabeth Parchment

Annetta Probst

PRENTICE HALL GINN CANADA

Contents

Bibliography

ME I AM!

by Jack Prelutsky
Photographed by Peter Chou

I am the only ME I AM
who qualifies as me;
no ME I AM has been before,
and none will ever be.

No other ME I AM can feel
the feelings I've within;
no other ME I AM can fit
precisely in my skin.

There is no other ME I AM
who thinks the thoughts I do;
the world contains one ME I AM,
there is no room for two.

I am the only ME I AM
this earth shall ever see;
that ME I AM I always am
is no one else but ME!

Jack Prelutsky started out as an opera singer and then sang folk songs in coffee shops before he began to write poetry. As a child he thought that poetry was "dull." When he later decided to become a poet, he realized that poetry could also be funny, exciting, and imaginative. Jack writes about everything from imaginary animals to everyday people and problems, like the bully down the block or being afraid of the dark. When he's not writing poems, he likes to ride his bicycle, make up word games, and collect model frogs.

All the colors of the race

by Arnold Adoff
Illustrated by Marc Mongeau

All the colors of the race
are
            in my face, and just behind my face:
                        behind my eyes:
            inside my head.

And inside my head, I give my self a place
      at the end of a long
                        line   forming
                              it self into a
                                    circle.

And I am holding out my hands.

ABOUT THE AUTHOR

ARNOLD ADOFF

In addition to being a poet, editor, and award-winning author, Arnold Adoff is also a legendary teacher. He now travels around the country reading his poems and working with young writers in their schools. His advice to writers is, "If you really want to write, you must read, read, read." Arnold is married to author Virginia Hamilton.

My Family

What My Family Means to Me

My family is important to me and I love them very much. I'm glad I have a big family. We depend on each other and enjoy being with each other.

How My Family Is Special

We have a lot of people in our family. Almost everybody is Italian. I speak English, French, and a little bit of Italian. My dad speaks Italian, Spanish, Portuguese, English, and a little bit of French. My mom speaks English and Italian. Everybody in my family speaks Italian. I have 23 cousins, 11 aunts, 10 uncles, one grandmother, and one grandfather.

Nicolina Mancuso

Age 9

I love to read both English and French books. I like swimming, hiking, and all family activities. I wrote "My Family" to let my family know how much I love them.

Nicolina Mancuso

Illustration by Matthew Rondina, age 12

Uncle Roger

My Uncle Roger is as tall as a giraffe,
As skinny as a toothpick,
As funny as a clown in the circus.
His hair's so funny it looks like
He stuck his finger in a light socket.
Jolly Roger!

Trever Taras
Grade 5

8

In Honor of Our Elders

In honor of our Elders, I would like to write about my grandmothers. I am very lucky to have two wonderful grandmothers. They are Grannie Hattie (Knott) and Granny Rosella (Shilling). My Grannie Hattie taught me all different kinds of crafts and how to play the organ.

My Granny Rosella always liked to play with my sister and me. We played old games and she taught us new games. She used to have races with us and she would always let us win.

My grannies would always make me laugh and give me a kiss and a hug when I asked questions. When there were important things happening, they took me to them and they taught me how to talk Indian and how to cook. So to me, honoring our Elders is honoring and loving the things my grandmothers gave and taught me.

Jeanette Knott
Grade 5

What Is a Grandparent ?

A grandma is sort of a mom, but is older. Some live with you and some don't.
Jack Thieu
Grade 4

A grandma and a grandpa spoil you, care if you are hurt, sometimes take care of you, love you always, and are nice to you.
Lynh Huynh
Grade 4

A nonna is your mommy's mom.

Marco Derosa,
Grade 4

A GRANDPARENT IS A PERSON WHO REALLY CARES ABOUT YOU.

CINDY FIDDLER
GRADE 4

My older friend is special and kind. She treats me different and takes me places.

Vanessa Weeseekase
Grade 4

Fox Song

by Joseph Bruchac
Illustrated by Paul Morin

The sun came slanting in through the window at the foot of Jamie's bed. She felt it on her face, but she didn't want to open her eyes. She knew what she would have to remember when she opened her eyes. She felt so alone. Perhaps now if she kept her eyes closed, she might be able to find her way back into the dream where Grama Bowman was with her.

There were so many things that she and Grama Bowman did together. It had been that way ever since Jamie could remember. Grama Bowman was actually her great-grandmother. She was Abenaki Indian and the mother of Jamie's mother's mother, and she was over ninety years old when she came to live with them in their house on the Winooski River, with the maple woods up the hill behind them. Such a long time ago, Jamie thought, six whole years. Most of my life. But not long enough. She kept her eyes closed, hearing Grama Bowman's voice telling her stories, seeing pictures in her mind of the things Grama Bowman and she loved to do together.

She saw them walking up Fox Hill in the heat of summer toward the slopes where the blackberries grew wild. Together they would pick out the berries that were, as Grama put it, "Just a little too ripe for us to take back, so we have to eat them here." Those berries were always the sweetest ones. Jamie remembered Grama explaining to her how their old people always cared for *alniminal*, the wild berries.

"They took care of them for hundreds of years before your father's people came here from France," Grama said.

"Your father's people were good people. They learned from us that you have to burn off the dead bushes each year so that the new ones will be green and strong." Grama Bowman smiled. "His people were quick to learn, and we were ready to teach them. I think that is why we have kept on marrying them all these years." Jamie nodded and smiled, even though she was not quite sure what the joke was. She knew it was one of those things that Grama Bowman told her to hold on to and remember because the knowing of it would come to her when she was a little older.

The sun's warmth was even stronger on her face now. Jamie heard her mother come into the room and stand by the bed. Her shadow was cool across Jamie's face, but Jamie lay still, knowing her mother would not bother her. Her mother's soft steps went out of the room. Jamie looked for another memory and found them walking along the river until they came to the grove of birch trees. It was spring and the trees were green with buds.

Grama Bowman put her hand on the trunk of one of the trees. "You see this mark here?" she said, pointing to the shape on the bark that looked almost like a bird. "We Abenaki say this is the mark of Badogi, the Thunder. The lightning is his arrow and he shoots it during the storms. But he doesn't want to hurt our people and so he marked these trees. Lightning never strikes these birch trees, so if you have to be near any tree in a storm, better to be near a young birch tree."

Jamie looked up and nodded. "I understand, Grama."

Grama Bowman took some tobacco from her pouch and placed it near the base of the tree. "Brother, we are going to take some of your clothing," she said to the tree.

"We thank you for this piece of your blanket." Grama Bowman smiled at Jamie. "You know, that is our Indian name for the birch. We call it *maskwa*, blanket tree." She took her knife and made a cut straight down the bark.

"We don't take too much so the tree won't die, Grama?"

"That is the way, Granddaughter, our old Indian way. Be careful what we take and only take what we need.

Now," she said, "you help me pull. We must go this way, to the left. The same direction the sun goes around the sky."

The basket they had made that day, using spruce roots to sew it together after folding it and making holes with Grama Bowman's bone awl, was sitting on Jamie's table near her bed. She opened her eyes for a moment to look at it, and she could still see the patterns on the basket that her grandmother had made. The shapes of birds and ferns and animals. And her grandmother's bone awl was in that basket now. She hadn't understood why Grama Bowman had given it to her from her bag when she last saw her.  Now she knew. She closed her eyes again, looking for her grandmother's face.

Grama Bowman's feet crunched through the snow in her white snow boots as they started on the trail to the maple grove up Fox Hill. Those boots were so big that the first time Jamie put them on—when she was a little girl—she couldn't move in them without falling. Grama Bowman always pretended that she couldn't remember which pair was hers and which was Jamie's. She would sit and struggle to put on Jamie's little galoshes while Jamie would stand in Grama's, giggling and saying,

"Grama, I really think that these may be yours!" Finally they would have their galoshes on and they would finish the tea that Jamie's mother always insisted they drink before going out to check on the trees.

"Warm inside, warm outside," Jamie's mother said.

"You see, Granddaughter," Grama Bowman said, "that is the way the circle of life goes. You take care of your children when they are little ones and when you get old your children will take care of you. And they will tell you what to do, too!" The way she said it made everyone smile. Grama Bowman had a way of pursing up her face that would make her look like a little girl.

Then they went out into the late winter snow and up the trail toward the maple grove. All along the way Grama would point things out, the way the ice had formed on the twigs, the places where deer had browsed on the trees, the tracks of the animals. She loved to tell Jamie the stories those tracks told her. Listening to Grama's words, Jamie could see the animals as if they were still there.

"Old Owl, Kokohas, he dove down right there for Madegwas, the Rabbit," Grama said. "You see his wing marks on the snow? But Rabbit, he was too quick."

As they walked along, there was one set of tracks that Grama Bowman especially loved to see. "Look," she would say, "those are the prints of my best friend, Wokwses, the Fox. She is a clever one. I know her tracks well. Now she is out looking for her old man. She wants to have some little ones for the spring. Sometime," Grama Bowman said, "when you are out here and I am not with you, you keep your eyes open. You might see her and when you do, you will think of me."

Jamie nodded but she wasn't sure that she understood. She couldn't imagine being in the woods without Grama by her side.

It was another half a kilometre beyond that clearing where they saw the tracks of the fox that they came to the line of trees that Jamie's father tapped for maple syrup. He would be along later in the morning with his tractor to collect the sap, but Grama always insisted that it was important for the two of them to come out whenever they could, just to make sure things were going right.

"We have to taste this sap and see that it is good," Grama Bowman said. She unhooked one of the buckets and tilted it so that Jamie could drink. There was nothing as light and subtly sweet as that taste.

Jamie opened her eyes and blinked away the tears. She closed her eyes again, afraid that she would no longer be able to see her grandmother in her memory.

But instead she found herself walking beside her along the hillslope. It was autumn, the leaves blowing in the wind, and it was very early in the morning. The sun was just coming up.

"My old Indian people," Grama Bowman said, "told me that the leaves love to dance. But they can only do their best dancing when they are ready to give themselves to the wind. That is when they are old, but they are the most beautiful then. They put on their best colors and then they dance."

A leaf came drifting past them and it brushed Jamie's face. It spiralled in the wind, went up and down, and then it touched the earth.

"When I see the leaves," Grama Bowman said, "I see my old people and remember they are still with me. We say that those who have gone are no further away from us than the leaves that have fallen."

The sun was a red arc lifting over the ridge and Grama reached out for Jamie's hand. "I brought you here to teach you a song. I forgot to teach it to my own daughter. But I know that you'll remember this song.

It is a welcoming song and it says hello to the new day. It says hello to every new person you meet and it welcomes them. When you sing it, you will not be alone."

Grama Bowman began to tap her open palm on her leg as they sat there in the fallen leaves, facing the east. In a clear high voice she sang:

Hey, kwah nu deh
Hey, kwah nu deh, kwah nu deh
Hey, kwah nu deh
Hey, kwah nu deh, kwah nu deh
Hey, hey, kwah nu deh

She sang it twice and the second time she sang it, Jamie sang with her. By the time they finished, the sun was up and its warmth was on their faces.

Jamie opened her eyes and sat up. She felt the sun on her face and she got out of bed. She hadn't taken her clothes off from the night before, and her mother had come in and covered her as she lay on the bed. She went out of her room, past her grandmother's empty room. She went downstairs and walked through the kitchen. Her mother and father were there, but they said nothing to her. She loved them for that understanding. She took her light jacket from its peg near the back door and went outside.

As soon as she reached the path she began to run, her feet scattering the leaves that gleamed yellow and red in the October morning light. When she reached the slope that looked over their house toward the east, she leaned back against the same tree where Grama Bowman used to sit, and faced the sun. She took four deep breaths and the racing of her heart slowed. Then, still facing the sun, she began to sing:

> Hey, kwah nu deh
> Hey, kwah nu deh, kwah nu deh

Something moved at the edge of her vision and she turned her head slowly. A meadowlark came flying out of the bushes at the edge of the clearing. Then, a few steps behind it, a small dog came walking out. It stood perfectly still. Jamie saw it wasn't a dog after all, it was a fox. It was as if it was waiting for something. Jamie began to sing again:

Hey, kwah nu deh
Hey, kwah nu deh, kwah nu deh
Hey, kwah nu deh

The fox yawned and sat down on its haunches. The sunlight was bright on its coat and its eyes glistened. Jamie continued the song:

Hey, kwah nu deh
Hey, kwah nu deh, kwah nu deh
Hey, kwah nu deh
Hey, kwah nu deh, kwah nu deh
Hey, hey, kwah nu deh

Jamie finished the song and looked away from the fox. She closed her eyes, feeling the warmth of the sun, which touched her face and touched the earth. When she opened her eyes again, the fox was gone. Had it really been there? She didn't know, but as she rose and went back down the hill, she knew that she would never be alone.

ABOUT THE AUTHOR — JOSEPH BRUCHAC

Joseph Bruchac always knew he would be a writer some day. His grandfather, an Abenaki Indian, taught the young Joseph how to fish and how to walk quietly through the woods. In his grandparents' general store, he sat by the wood stove and listened to farmers and lumberjacks tell tall tales. Joseph began his writing career by writing poems for his second-grade teacher. Much later, when he left home to go to college, he began to look for Native elders who could tell him the traditional stories. He started writing them down when he had children of his own to pass them on to. He offers this advice to anyone who wants to become a writer: "You have to do it one page at a time, and you have to keep on doing it. You take one step to climb a mountain."

"What Are You Doing, Grandpa?"

by Jamila Gavin
Illustrated by Tadeusz Majewski

Neetu and her little brother Sanjay have two grandpas—Mom's dad and Dad's dad.

Mom's dad lives in India and they have never ever seen him. But Dad's dad lives in Leicester and they see him quite often.

Although they love and respect Dad's dad, as head of the family, Neetu and Sanjay are a little afraid of him. Whenever he comes to visit, they all have to be on their toes.

If Neetu wears jeans, Grandpa Leicester frowns at her and snorts, "I don't like my granddaughter wearing jeans," so she has to go and put on a dress. If Sanjay, who is a terrible chatterbox, sometimes interrupts, Grandfather glares at him sternly and says, "I don't like little boys who interrupt," and Sanjay has to bite his lip and try so hard not to speak.

When their mother got a job and went out to work, Grandfather was very disapproving. "I don't like my daughter-in-law going out to work." Mom just smiled politely, and went anyway, and Dad took his father aside to try to explain how with Mom going to work, they could afford a new car.

Perhaps the worst time is when Dad's dad comes to stay and they can't eat their favorite pizza and chips. Instead, they have to eat vegetable curry, runny spinach with eggs, and horrible stuff like that.

One day, Mom said excitedly, "Children! Your grandpa is coming to stay! Isn't that wonderful!" But they didn't think it was wonderful at all. Neetu just groaned and said, "Oh no! I'll have to wear nothing but dresses," and Sanjay moaned, "Oh no! We'll have to eat curried eggs."

It was Dad who beamed at them and said, "It's not my dad from Leicester who's coming to visit us, it's your Mom's dad from Calcutta. You've never met him! You can call him 'Grandpa Chatterji'."

Neetu and Sanjay looked at each other doubtfully. How could they know whether a grandad from Calcutta was any different from a grandad from Leicester, even if he was called Grandpa Chatterji? They would just have to wait and see.

All that week Mom went round with a smile on her face, and even Dad seemed quite relaxed. Mom got the spare room ready, just as she always did for Dad's dad. But instead of worriedly scrubbing and cleaning and polishing and checking that there was not one speck of dust to be seen anywhere in the house, she actually hummed and sang and seemed to enjoy making everything look nice.

On the day of his arrival, Mom and Dad got up very early and drove off to the airport to meet Grandpa Chatterji. Neetu and Sanjay didn't go because there wouldn't be room in the car on the way back. Old Mrs. Bennet from next door came in to look after them.

They waited and waited. Sanjay looked out of one window and Neetu looked out of the other. What would he be like? Would he wear a smart suit and shiny black shoes like Dad's dad? Would he smoke cigars and sit in the best easy chair and talk business with Dad in a big boomy voice? Would he have the best bed? Would he be served first at the table? Would he always insist on using the bathroom first in the morning, even though he took the longest and made them late for school? And would he be critical and strict and insist on total obedience at all times?

They waited and waited. Suddenly, Sanjay shouted, "They're here!" The little red Mini had pulled up outside the house.

"Oh dear," cried Neetu, suddenly going all shy, "I'm going to hide."

They both hid behind the sofa. They heard the front door open. They heard Mom come in and say gently, "Welcome to our home!" They heard Dad say, "I'll take your luggage up to your room," and they heard a thin, quiet, soft voice say, "And where are my little grandchildren?"

Then there was silence. Crouched behind the sofa, Neetu and Sanjay hardly breathed. Then suddenly, although they didn't hear Grandpa Chatterji come into the room, they knew he was there because they saw a pair of bare, dark-brown, knobbly, long-toed, bony feet.

The feet came and stood right close by them. The feet emerged from beneath thin, white trousers, and as their eyes travelled all the way up, past a white tunic and brown waistcoat and past a red and blue woolly scarf round the neck, they found themselves looking into a round, shining, kind, wrinkly face, with deep-as-oceans large, brown eyes, and a mass of pure, white, fluffy hair which fell in a tangle over his brow.

"Ah!" exclaimed Grandpa Chatterji with a great, loving sigh, and he opened his arms to embrace them.

After they had all hugged each other, Mom said, "Children, take Grandpa up to his room, he will want to bathe and change after his long journey. I'll go and make a nice cup of tea."

Sanjay began chattering as he clambered up the stairs, leading the way.

"Why aren't you wearing any shoes?" he asked.

"Because I took them off at the door, so as not to bring any dirt into the house. We always do that in India," answered Grandpa Chatterji.

"Did you come with lots of suitcases, Grandpa?" Sanjay went on, "and did you bring us lots of presents?"

"Ssh!" said Neetu, embarrassed. "That's rude, Sanjay."

"Just you wait and see," replied Grandpa, who didn't mind at all.

When they went into the guest room, they couldn't see any suitcases at all.

"Where is your luggage?" asked Neetu.

"Oh, I only ever travel with my bedroll," said Grandpa. "My needs are very simple," and he pointed to a roly-poly round khaki, canvas roll, all held together with leather straps, and covered in airline stickers and labels.

"Does that mean we don't have presents?" sighed Sanjay.

"Just you wait and see," replied Grandpa again.

"You've got the best room in the house," chattered Sanjay, bravely trying to ignore the mysterious roll which contained everything that Grandpa had brought.

"You've got the nicest sheets with duvet and curtains to match, you have the plumpiest pillows and the softest bed. It's the best bed in the house for bouncing on," and Sanjay flung himself onto the bed, which Mom had made all smooth and neat, and he rumpled it all up.

"Sanjay!" cried Neetu with horror, dragging him off.

"Look what you've done," and she tried to straighten it out.

"If you like this bed so much, you'd better sleep in it," said Grandpa Chatterji. "I prefer something harder."

"Where will you sleep then, Grandpa?" asked Neetu looking worried.

"I'll sleep on the floor as I always do" he replied. "I am like a snail, my dear," murmured Grandpa. "All I need, wherever I go, is my bedroll. It carries all my belongings, and when I unroll it, it becomes my bed."

The children looked in awe at the khaki, canvas roll. It suddenly seemed to be the most important thing in the world. "Can we unroll it, Grandpa?" whispered Sanjay.

Grandpa bent over the roll and undid the old leather straps, then he slowly unrolled it alongside the bed. At first it seemed that all it contained was one sheet and one blanket. Sanjay was sure there were no presents; but then Grandpa wriggled his hand into the large pocket at one end of the roll and pulled out a tooth mug and toothbrush all wrapped in a towel, a hairbrush and comb, and his shaving things. Sanjay stared expectantly. Were there any presents?

Then Grandpa went to a pocket at the other end and wriggled his hand inside. He pulled out a woolly jumper, a woolly hat, some socks, underwear, hankies, a shirt, tunic, and waistcoat, but still no presents.

At last, he folded back the sheet. Between the sheet and the blanket was a small, faded rug. He pulled back the rug to show lots of different packages.

"Presents!" breathed Sanjay, full of expectation.

"Why did you bring that old rug?" asked Neetu in a puzzled voice.

Grandpa Chatterji lifted it out as though it were the most precious thing in the world. "I never go anywhere without this," he murmured. "It is my meditation rug. I sit on it to do all my thinking and praying."

"Are those things presents?" asked Sanjay, pointing to the packages.

"Yes, yes, here you are," laughed Grandpa. He handed Sanjay two long thin packages.

"Thank you, thank you!" yelled Sanjay, ripping them open. "What are they?"

"One is a specially made, wooden wriggly snake, and the other is an Indian flute. Later I will teach you some tunes, but for now, you can just blow. It makes a lovely sound. Snakes love the sound of the flute. It makes them sway and puts them into a good mood."

Sanjay flung his arms round his old grandfather. "Thank you, thank you, Grandpa Chatterji!" and he rushed off to show his mom and dad.

Neetu waited patiently. Which package was for her? He bent over and handed her one of the larger ones. "What a beauty you are, my dearest, little granddaughter! This is for you."

When Neetu opened up her package, she found a beautiful pink and green and gold sari. It was a special small-sized sari for little girls. In India they have to wait until they are nearly grown-up before they can wear a sari, but all little girls love to have a sari they can dress up in, and this is what her grandfather had brought for her.

It made Neetu feel very solemn and proud. "Oh thank you, Grandpa!" she declared in a grown-up voice, "I'll go and ask Mom to help me put it on."

Later, when Grandpa Chatterji had bathed and changed, Neetu, all dressed up in her sari, and Sanjay, with his snake and flute, went upstairs to find him. They knocked on his door.

"Come in!" he said in his soft, high voice.

They went in. Grandpa was sitting on the floor on his old rug. He was sitting very straight, his eyes staring in front and his arms stretched over his cross-legged knees.

"What are you doing, Grandpa?" asked Sanjay.

"I'm being a lotus flower floating quietly on a sea of milk."

"Why are you being a lotus flower?" asked Neetu. She was looking like such a beautiful, grown-up lady in her new sari.

Grandpa looked at her and smiled with admiration. "Come, children. Come and sit next to me. There's room on the rug."

Neetu and Sanjay sat cross-legged, one on each side of their grandfather. They stretched out their arms over their knees and straightened their backs.

"We are being lotus flowers because we are trying to be as calm and peaceful and perfect as lotus flowers are," explained Grandpa Chatterji, "and if you close your eyes, you can imagine you are floating on a sea of milk before the creation of the world."

The children closed their eyes and floated away.

Then Grandpa suddenly woke up with a shout and cried, "I feel rested now! Come on! Where's that cup of tea your mother promised me? And while I'm drinking my tea, Sanjay can play the flute, and Neetu can dance! Will you?" he begged, his dark eyes glittering.

Neetu and Sanjay nodded with excitement. "Oh, Grandpa Chatterji! We're so glad you came."

ABOUT THE AUTHOR   JAMILA GAVIN

Jamila Gavin was born in India. Her father was Indian and her mother was English. Jamila believes that growing up with parents from two different cultures has had a lasting effect on her writing.

As a child, Jamila loved writing, composing music, dancing, and acting. She has studied music in England, France, and Germany, and has also worked in radio and TV.

Brothers and Sisters

Photographed by Peter Chou

Rajiv's Journal

September 6

I can't write anything about brothers, because I don't have any. I'm an expert on sisters, though. My twin sisters, Saira and Indira, are just four. I have to admit that they're pretty cute. They follow me around a lot, and they're always asking me to read them stories. I don't mind doing that, actually. I kind of like reading in funny voices and making them giggle.

Yesterday, though, something awful happened. The twins got into my science project while I was at school. I'd worked really hard making a model volcano. It was awesome, and I could hardly wait to bring it to school for the science fair. Well, the twins fooled around with it and set it off—all over my desk. Yuck, what a mess! Now I have to start my project all over again. I like my sisters most of the time, but right now I'd rather have gerbils!

September 10

Here's what I like about being the youngest in my family:

1. I probably get more hugs than my brother and sister.
2. My parents don't yell at me if I make a mess.
3. I don't have to take out the garbage.
4. When I really, really wanted a kitten, my dad said I could have one, even though he doesn't like cats.

What *don't* I like? Well, maybe just a few things:

1. My older brother and sister always leave me out of what they're doing.
2. My parents make me go to bed when everyone else can stay up.
3. I hardly ever get to pick what we watch on TV.
4. I don't get as much allowance as my brother and sister.

That's funny. My lists came out even!

Michael's Journal

SEPTEMBER 18

BEING THE MIDDLE KID IN A FAMILY CAN BE PRETTY COOL SOMETIMES. OTHER TIMES IT'S NOT. HERE'S WHAT I MEAN. THERE ARE FIVE KIDS IN MY FAMILY. MY TWO OLDER BROTHERS THINK I'M A LITTLE GUY. SOMETIMES THEY'RE REALLY GREAT TO ME. FOR INSTANCE, MY OLDEST BROTHER, TIM, IS A PITCHER IN THE LITTLE LEAGUE AND HE'S SHOWING ME ALL HIS PITCHING TRICKS. PETER, MY NEXT OLDEST BROTHER, IS A COMPUTER NUT, AND HE LETS ME PLAY GAMES WITH HIM. OTHER TIMES, THOUGH, TIM AND PETER GO OFF TOGETHER, AND LEAVE ME OUT. THEY WON'T LET ME HANG OUT WITH THEIR FRIENDS, EITHER.

WITH MY YOUNGER BROTHER AND SISTER, IT'S A WHOLE DIFFERENT THING. THEY THINK I'M A BIG GUY, AND THEY ALWAYS WANT ME TO PLAY WITH THEM. WELL, I DO SOMETIMES, JUST TO BE NICE. I GET PRETTY TIRED OF THEIR LITTLE-KID GAMES, THOUGH, AND SOMETIMES I WISH THEY DIDN'T TAG ALONG AFTER ME SO MUCH!

BEING A MIDDLE KID IS KIND OF INTERESTING. IT'S ALMOST LIKE BEING TWO DIFFERENT PEOPLE AT THE SAME TIME.

September 30

We're supposed to write about our brothers and sisters. The thing is, I don't have any—I'm an only kid. Most of the time I think that's fine. My parents always have time for me, and I don't have to share them with other kids.

My friend Ari has a brother and a sister. When I go over to his place, I can't help noticing how different it is when there are other kids in a family. You have to share things more. Ari also doesn't get as much new stuff as I do. Boy, I'd hate that!

Sometimes, though, I can't help thinking it might be nice to have a brother or a sister. Then, when your parents are being really unfair, you'd have someone to agree with you and back you up. You'd also have someone to play with whenever you wanted.

Still, I'm pretty lucky being just the way I am, the only kid in my family.

October 4

My sister Mariah is four years older than I am. Mostly we get along okay. When our parents want us to do something really boring it's great to have someone to moan and groan with. She's smart, too, and she helps me with my homework. That makes me feel good.

Riah's no angel, though. Yesterday I borrowed her best T-shirt. Well, I did forget to ask. Then I spilled juice on it. Not a whole lot, but you should have heard her yell! Then she spun her wheelchair around and just zoomed out of the kitchen. I started to cry, and Mom called after her, "Let's not fuss about it, Riah. JaNette didn't mean to spoil your shirt." Of course I didn't! I don't see why she gets so angry about stuff like that.

There definitely are good things and bad things about sisters!

October 22

Mom married her boyfriend Don last year. That's when his two kids came to live with us. I call them "the steps," because they're my stepbrother and stepsister. I was worried about living with "the steps," but things have worked out okay. Kevin's quite old, almost sixteen, so he doesn't bother me much. He works weekends at Hamburger Heaven, and when we go there to eat he gives me a big wink and puts double pickle on my burger, just the way I like it. Lisa is twelve, just three years older than I am, and she dresses really cool. I like to hang around and watch her get dressed so I can learn how to do it too.

Some things about "the steps" bother me, though. It would be nice if Kevin could talk about something besides basketball. He calls me Short Stuff, too, and that bugs me. Lisa can be pretty bossy, and she makes a big fuss if I go in her room when she isn't there. Sometimes, too, Mom calls her "my big girl," and that makes me feel funny inside.

The "steps" aren't always easy to live with, but they're interesting!

Mina's Journal

OCTOBER 13

MOST OF THE TIME, I REALLY LIKE BEING THE OLDEST KID IN MY FAMILY. I GET TO STAY UP LATER THAN MY YOUNGER BROTHERS, AND I GET LOTS MORE ALLOWANCE. I GET TO TELL THEM WHAT TO DO, TOO. BEING THE OLDEST ISN'T ALWAYS EASY, THOUGH. MY DAD'S A SINGLE PARENT, AND HE REALLY DEPENDS ON ME TO HELP OUT. BECAUSE I'M OLDEST, I'M NOT SUPPOSED TO DO ANYTHING WRONG, EVER. I ALSO HAVE TO LOOK AFTER MY BROTHERS QUITE A LOT. WHEN THEY GOOF OFF, I GET BLAMED BECAUSE I DIDN'T STOP THEM. MY BROTHERS GET MORE FUN OUT OF DOING DUMB STUFF BECAUSE THEY KNOW I'LL GET IN TROUBLE TOO.

I GUESS IF I HAD TO CHOOSE, THOUGH, I'D STILL WANT TO BE THE OLDEST!

I Wish I Were the Oldest

by R. Ward Riley
Illustrated by Scot Ritchie

I wish I were the oldest like Larry. He always gets what I want. Like the time I wanted a ten-speed bike. I had looked at them in the store and marked where they were in the catalogue. But what happens? When my brother's birthday comes along, *he* gets the bike I wanted.

I wish I were the oldest.

I really want a pet. I know we can't have a cat or a dog because we live in an apartment, but I still want a pet. I've been to the pet shop and looked at the hamsters and gerbils. I've even looked at the turtles, but they aren't much to pet.

Mom finally says we can have a pet if it stays in a cage on our desk and doesn't make too much noise. Mom also says she isn't going to pay for it. If we want a pet, we have to earn some money. But it's my brother who gets the job cleaning Grandma's garage, and *he* gets paid.

I tell Grandma I wish I were the oldest.

Larry has brought his pet home today and won't let me into the room until everything is all set up. I hang around the kitchen telling Mom I wish I were the oldest.

Finally the bedroom door opens, and Mom, Dad, and I are allowed in. There on the desk under a lamp is a glass cage with rocks, sand, plastic plants—and a snake!

My dad says, "Interesting."

My mom says, "Keep it in the cage."

I ask, "What does it eat?"

"Mice," Larry answers, holding up a jar with holes in the lid and a tiny white mouse inside.

My dad says, "Interesting."

My mom says, "Keep it in the jar."

I say, "It has pink eyes."

All my brother's friends are real impressed that Larry has a snake. Everyone talks about it. Everyone wants to touch it. Everyone wants Larry to feed it. I tell everyone I wish I were the oldest and had a snake. "Here, little mouse," I whisper, standing near the jar, "you can eat the rest of my cookie."

The tiny mouse holds the crumbs in his paws to eat them. When he finishes, he washes his face and ears. No one notices when I lift the mouse out of the jar and hold him close to my chest. He hardly moves, but I can feel his heart beating. He is very quiet. I think he likes me.

Mom's voice interrupts us, "School tomorrow. Better get ready for bed."

Our friends go home, and the snake's cage is closed. Larry is stuffing his books and papers into his book bag. "Get your stuff off the desk." He doesn't notice that I'm holding the tiny mouse. I push my spelling paper into my bag and gently put the mouse in under it. There are plenty of crumbs to eat in the bottom.

I fall asleep thinking of the way the mouse felt in my hand.

In the morning I wake up to the sound of my mother yelling, "The mouse is loose. Larry, you find that mouse—*or else!*"

Larry jumps out of bed and examines the glass jar. It's empty.

He scrambles around on the floor, looking behind the beds, the desk, and in the closet.

"Gotta find that mouse," he says. "Mom is going to be furious."

I quickly get out of bed, get dressed, and take my book bag to the kitchen for breakfast. On the way to school I slip a crust of toast into the bag just in case "Pinkie" is hungry.

In the classroom I carefully hang my book bag on a hook where no one will bump into it. I reach into the bag and touch the mouse before pulling out my spelling paper.

"Oh no!" Part of the paper is gone. I hurry back to my seat. When we hand our homework in, I put my paper on the bottom of the stack. Maybe the teacher won't notice.

"Andrew," the teacher says. "Please come here." I walk slowly to her desk.

"What happened to your paper?"

"What paper?"

"This paper with no bottom."

"Maybe a mouse ate it."

"H'm. And where is this mouse?"

"It could be in my book bag."

"I think you should show me this homework-eating mouse."

I can tell by the look on her face that she doesn't believe me.

I reach into my bag and gently pull out the mouse.

Sitting on the hard bench outside the principal's office, my book bag on my lap, I can feel my eyes stinging. So I tell myself that if I were the oldest, I wouldn't feel like crying. I can feel the mouse scratching around inside the bag.

Finally the principal comes and leads me into her office and asks me what has happened. I tell her there is a mouse in my book bag, but she says she doesn't want to see it. She starts telling me the school rules and serious trouble stuff. My eyes start stinging again, and I don't hear a lot of what she says until ". . . your mother will be here soon." Boy, I *am* in serious trouble.

My eyes start watering then, and the principal hands me a tissue and tells me to sit on the bench.

My mom doesn't look too happy when she arrives at the principal's office. Or when she comes out. We walk to the car, and I sit in the front seat, holding my book bag. I give a few loud sniffs and keep blowing my nose to make her less angry at me.

Between sniffs I tell her I wish I were the oldest like Larry.

Mom reminds me that Larry is in a lot of trouble for losing the mouse. I have to tell her the mouse isn't lost—it's in my book bag. I think she already knows, because she starts laughing instead of yelling.

"His name is Pinkie, because he has pink eyes," I tell her. I fish around the bottom of my bag until I catch him, then I let him sit on my hand. Mom points out that he has tiny toenails and that he sniffs all the time with his tiny pink nose. I tell her I like the way his tail curls round my fingers. And can I please keep him?

As fast as I can, I tell her how I'll take care of him. How he can eat my bread crusts and I'll keep him in my book bag and he'll never, never get loose.

Mom agrees with everything except the part about Pinkie living in my book bag. Now he lives in a little wire cage with a water bottle.

Larry's snake is eating crickets now. They live in the same jar with holes in the lid that used to be Pinkie's. Larry's in big trouble, because Dad just found one of the crickets in the shower. Today I'm glad I'm me.

ABOUT THE

ILLUSTRATOR   SCOT RITCHIE

Scot Ritchie decided he wanted to be an artist when he was just a child. He created greeting cards for ten years, developing a style that uses simple, expressive lines with lively color. He has illustrated fourteen children's books and also does work for newspapers, magazines, and advertising. What Scot enjoys most about his job is the opportunity to draw humorous characters and situations.

Ten Ways of Driving Your Sister Batty

1. Borrow her clothes and don't return them.
2. Always talk on the phone when she's expecting a phone call.
3. Sing off-key in front of her.
4. Chew your food loudly.
5. Watch a TV program that she doesn't like.
6. Make fun of her cooking.
7. Use her favorite CD for second base.
8. Trade her for six hockey cards.
9. Wash your goldfish in the sink.
10. Put food coloring in her shampoo.

Cathy Roslund
Peter O'Meara

Grade 9

Kid , Kids , Kids

Kids at the window,
Kids at the door,
Tiny in the baby seat
Toddler on the floor.

Helping in the kitchen,
Running up the stair,
An overflowing small house,
And not a kid to spare.

Sharon Bahry
Age 10

Little Brother

B — Bugs me
O — Often changes the TV channel
T — Takes my turn at Sega
H — Hits me
E — Eats my candy
R — Runs away with my money

Put that together and you spell **BOTHER.**
And that's what my little brother usually is.
But I left out a very important letter.

R — Really, my best bud.

Jamie Mackie
Age 9

My interest in writing started back in kindergarten. I kept choosing the centre where you drew a picture and told someone what to write about it. I wrote this poem about my brother in a restaurant when I was having lunch with my grandma, but mostly I write on the computer.

Christopher and Jamie Mackie

Families

by Lynn Bryan

T.J.

T.J.'S BROTHER and older sisters gave him his name. T.J. was born into their family after their mother got remarried. When they went to see him in the hospital, they were told that his name was Terence John. "Hi, T.J.!" they said. And that name stuck.

"I'm glad Mom already had kids," says T.J. "I always had someone to play with or look after me. I kept them pretty busy because I was always getting into something.

"When I was little, I liked to go down into my brother Andrew's room while he was at school. I'd bring his toys up and hide them in my room. Now I try to beat Andrew at video games; he's hard to beat. Andrew and I are five years apart; I'm nine and he's fourteen.

"Laura and Shannon are my sisters. They're both in high school, so they're pretty busy. They are good athletes—actually, all of us like sports.

"My mom graduated this fall, and we all went to the ceremony. I went up to sit with her, so I was the first one to see her diploma."

The Dunn family has a cottage at the lake named "Auld Reekie." "That's the nickname for Edinburgh, the city Dad's family came from in Scotland," explains T.J.

"There are lots of things for us to do out at the lake. My favorite thing is to go fishing. Two years ago, I caught my first fish—a fifty-centimetre pike. I got it to the dock and then my dad pulled it in. Boy, was I excited!

"Life would be pretty boring if it was just me around. I'm glad I have Andrew and Laura and Shannon, even if we do bug each other sometimes—maybe even a lot!"

Jamie

JAMIE doesn't have to go far to spend time with his grandparents, for they live right with him. His family discovered how much they enjoyed living together when they first shared a house just after Jamie was born.

"Now we live in a house close to my school—it's the same school my mom used to go to. Nani and Gramps have their bedroom and living room downstairs. I wake up earlier than my brother and sisters, so I often go downstairs and talk to Nani. She gets up early too. We talk lots, and sometimes we even have time to make crafts."

Counting his grandparents, there are eight people in Jamie's family. Jamie tells a bit about them.

"Kaitlin is three years younger than me. She's in Grade 1 and wishes she was the oldest so she could have gone to school a long time ago. She's always dancing and singing around the house. Now she's teaching my baby sister, Jocelyn, to do that too. There's not much room in the living room when they're twirling around.

"My little brother and I share a bedroom. That's good because we can put our hockey pictures up all over the walls. Christopher likes to copy the things I do—I like that. He plays with Kaitlin and Jocelyn too 'cause they're around more than me.

"I like hockey a lot. I play goal and my dad is one of our coaches. He's the best! I also take jazz dancing with my friend, John. I think it helps me in goal, because you have to be flexible and quick.

"My mom used to take jazz. But she's too busy now, helping out at my school and working. Sometimes she works at the office with Gramps. When they get home, we all have supper—my dad might make it, or maybe Nani.

"My big family is great! They make me feel good about myself. If I have a problem I can find somebody to talk to. And there's lots of people to come to my hockey games!"

BENITA WAS born in Canada. The rest of her family was born in a part of the world that is near the equator and very hot.

"My dad was born in Malaysia and my mom was born in Brunei. Both countries are part of the island of Borneo," Benita explains. "My brother was born in Brunei too. When Ben was just six months old, they moved to Canada. I was born about three years after that."

Benita goes on to say, "I went to a Chinese bilingual school in Edmonton from kindergarten to Grade 3. Ben went to Chinese bilingual school till Grade 6. We learned to speak and write Chinese quite well. This is my Chinese name, which means King of Jade Flower."

"Now we've moved to Calgary, and Ben and I just go to Chinese school on Saturday mornings. I have the best teacher in the school. She gives us extra recess time and she is always smiling.

"The school near our house is an English school. It has Grades 4 to 9. Mom and Dad decided to put us in that school because Ben and I could both go there together.

"That was good because, for a while, we didn't know anyone. It was hard to get new friends at first. And we missed our old friends.

"Just before we moved to Calgary, our family went to Brunei for my uncle's wedding. I was the flower girl and I wore a long pink dress. My brother was the best man. There were about a thousand people at the wedding.

"We were in Brunei for five weeks and had a nice holiday. We did a lot of swimming and visited relatives. I got to see my grandma and grandpa who live in Brunei. My other grandma lives in Edmonton.

"My mom and dad really care about us. They spend a lot of time with us. We play games together. We do quite a bit of cycling and we like to go camping in the summer.

"We live close to the mountains now, so we can ski together.

"I'm very happy."

Eric

ERIC WAS WELCOMED into the Betts family on the day he was born. It took three years, but finally, the adoption papers were signed. His mom excitedly told his sisters, "It's through! Eric's adopted!"

Little Eric chimed in with what he thought they said: "I'm a doctor!"

Eric tells about his family. "I have two big sisters; one's Shannon and one's Missy. Shannon has her own apartment now, and my dad and mom are divorced. So that means there's just Mom, me, and Missy in our house now. And my cat, Angel, too.

"Missy is in Grade 12. She wants to go to university, but it's too expensive. So, she thought of a plan. She started wrestling and got really good. Now she's a world-class wrestler, and has a scholarship to go to university.

"I'll be going to university, because I want to be a teacher. My Grade 4 teacher this year is so nice that I decided that's what I want to be. Maybe I can get a hockey scholarship—or a swimming one.

"My mom has a good job at a nursing home, but she had to go to school first. Sometimes when she had night classes and my sisters weren't home to babysit, I went with her.

"I don't get to see Shannon a lot; she's usually at work. She has two jobs, and sometimes three. Mostly I see her when we all meet over at my Grandma's for lunch or something."

Just a while ago, Eric gave his mom something special; something that brought tears to her eyes.

"I wrote Mom a letter and put it in our mailbox. She said that the words were so beautiful they made her cry." Here's part of the letter.

Thank you for my life and thankyou for adopting me.

Love Eric

"I really meant what I wrote. Sometimes I see the mother I was born to, but not very much—I don't need to. I love the family I've got, and they love me."

ROBIN AND HER older sister, Alexandra, live with their mother. Four years ago, when Robin was six, their dad remarried. His new wife had a daughter named Elizabeth. So then Robin had a stepsister as well as a sister.

Robin recalls the wedding. "It was exciting being in the wedding. I was a ring bearer; so was Alexandra. We carried the rings for Dad and Meg on pillows. Elizabeth was the flower girl.

"Being stepsisters hasn't been exactly easy. At first, it seemed funny to share our dad with Elizabeth. And she didn't liked sharing her mom with us. We used to argue about who got to sit beside Dad and who would sit beside Meg at the dinner table.

"Usually, we only see Elizabeth every second weekend, and you don't get to know someone very well that way. But we've had some holidays together now, and things have gotten better.

"We just got back from a wonderful holiday in Toronto. We went down there to visit Dad's family. My grandpa and grandma were born in Italy. Grandma can speak English, but our grandpa speaks only Italian. Grandma made lots of pasta and baked special Italian cookies.

"At our dad's, Alexandra has a room of her own. Elizabeth and I share a room with bunk beds. It is nice having company at night, especially if we have nightmares.

"It took Alexandra and Elizabeth and me quite a while to like each other, but now we feel like we belong together. When Dad told us that in a few weeks he will be able to adopt Elizabeth, we were all really excited! Now we'll really be sisters and we'll all have DiMarco for our last name.

"My dad loves all of us, and so does Meg. It seems kind of nice to share our parents now. Elizabeth says that our dad will also be her dad everyday, forever."

Fly Away Home

by Eve Bunting
Illustrated by Ronald Himler

My dad and I live in an airport. That's because we don't have a home and the airport is better than the streets. We are careful not to get caught.

Mr. Slocum and Mr. Vail were caught last night.

"Ten green bottles, hanging on the wall," they sang. They were as loud as two moose bellowing.

Dad says they broke the first rule of living here. Don't get noticed.

Dad and I try not to get noticed. We stay among the crowds. We change airlines.

"Delta, TWA, Northwest, we love them all," Dad says.

He and I wear blue jeans and blue T-shirts and blue jackets. We each have a blue zippered bag with a change of blue clothes. Not to be noticed is to look like nobody at all.

Once we saw a woman pushing a metal cart full of stuff. She wore a long, dirty coat and she lay down across a row of seats in front of Continental Gate 6. The cart, the dirty coat, the lying down were all noticeable. Security moved her out real fast.

Dad and I sleep sitting up. We use different airport areas.
"Where are we tonight?" I ask.

Dad checks his notebook. "Alaska Air," he says. "Over in the other terminal."

That's O.K. We like to walk.

We know some of the airport regulars by name and by sight. There's Idaho Joe and Annie Frannie and Mars Man. But we don't sit together.

"Sitting together will get you noticed faster than anything," Dad says.

Everything in the airport is on the move — passengers, pilots, flight attendants, cleaners with their brooms. Jets roar in, close to the windows.

Other jets roar out. Luggage bounces down chutes, escalators glide up and down, disappearing under floors. Everyone's going somewhere except Dad and me. We stay.

Once a little brown bird got into the main terminal and couldn't get out. It fluttered in the high, hollow spaces. It threw itself at the glass, fell panting on the floor, flew to a tall, metal girder, and perched there, exhausted.

"Don't stop trying," I told it silently. "Don't! You can get out!"

For days the bird flew around, dragging one wing. And then it found the instant when a sliding door was open and slipped through. I watched it rise. Its wing seemed O.K.

"Fly, bird," I whispered. "Fly away home!"

Though I couldn't hear it, I knew it was singing. Nothing made me as happy as that bird.

The airport's busy and noisy even at night. Dad and I sleep anyway. When it gets quiet, between two and four a.m., we wake up.

"Dead time," Dad says. "Almost no flights coming in or going out."

At dead time there aren't many people around, so we're extra careful.

In the mornings Dad and I wash up in one of the bathrooms, and he shaves. The bathrooms are crowded, no matter how early. And that's the way we like it.

Strangers talk to strangers.

"Where did you get in from?"

"Three hours our flight was delayed. Man! Am I bushed!"

Dad and I, we don't talk to anyone.

We buy doughnuts and milk for breakfast at one of the cafeterias, standing in line with our red trays. Sometimes Dad gets me a carton of juice.

On the weekends Dad takes the bus to work. He's a janitor in an office in the city. The bus fare's a dollar each way.

On those days Mrs. Medina looks out for me. The Medinas live in the airport, too — Grandma, Mrs. Medina, and Denny, who's my friend.

He and I collect rented luggage carts that people have left outside and return them for fifty cents each. If the crowds are big and safe, we offer to carry bags.

"Get this one for you, lady? It looks heavy."

Or, "Can I call you a cab?" Denny's real good at calling cabs. That's because he's seven already.

Sometimes passengers don't tip. Then Denny whispers, "Stingy!" But he doesn't whisper too loud. The Medinas understand that it's dangerous to be noticed.

When Dad comes home from work, he buys hamburgers for us and the Medinas. That's to pay them for watching out for me. If Denny and I've had a good day, we treat for pie. But I've stopped doing that. I save my money in my shoe.

"Will we ever have our own apartment again?" I ask Dad. I'd like it to be the way it was, before Mom died.

"Maybe we will," he says. "If I can find more work. If we can save some money." He rubs my head. "It's nice right here, though, isn't it, Andrew? It's warm. It's safe. And the price is right."

But I know he's trying all the time to find us a place. He takes newspapers from the trash baskets and makes pencil circles around letters and numbers. Then he goes to the phones. When he comes back he looks sad. Sad and angry. I know he's been calling about an apartment. I know the rents are too high for us.

"I'm saving money, too," I tell him, and I lift one foot and point to my shoe.

Dad smiles. "Atta boy!"

"If we get a place, you and your dad can come live with us," Denny says.

"And if *we* get a place, you and your mom and *your* grandma can come live with *us*," I say.

"Yeah!"

We shake on it. That's going to be so great!

After next summer, Dad says, I have to start school.

"How?" I ask.

"I don't know. But it's important. We'll work it out."

Denny's mom says he can wait for a while. But Dad says I can't wait.

Sometimes I watch people meeting people.

"We missed you."

"It's so good to be home."

Sometimes I get mad, and I want to run at them and push them and shout, "Why do *you* have homes when we don't? What makes

you so special?" That would get us
noticed, all right.

Sometimes I just want to cry. I think Dad
and I will be here forever.

Then I remember the bird. It took a while, but
a door opened. And when the bird left, when it flew free,
I know it was singing.

ABOUT THE AUTHOR   EVE BUNTING

Even though Eve Bunting didn't start writing until her
children were nearly grown, she has still managed to
write more than a hundred books! Eve's stories are about
everything from sharks to ghosts, but she especially likes
to write about Ireland, where she was born. Her advice to
children who would like to be writers is to read lots of books.
As a child, Eve's favorite story was *Anne of Green Gables*.

That Family Picnic Was Certainly Unusual

Our first family picnic this year was definitely unusual. When we arrived at the park, my mom realized that she had forgotten the lunch at home! We all shuffled back to the car, grumbled all the way home, and then set out again. We were halfway back to the park this time, when we realized we had left my sister in the house, so back we went again. We found her sitting forlornly on our back step wondering why she had been left behind. We all scrambled back into the car for the third time, hoping that we had our act together, but three blocks later we had a flat tire, which took half an hour for my dad to fix!

Arriving at the park, we were so hungry that we gobbled down our lunch. I must admit we did have fun, even though my sister chased a squirrel up a tree, and then was too scared to come down without my dad's assistance. We packed up our belongings and headed for home about 5:00, so tired we could hardly move and only wanted to rest when we got home. To our dismay we discovered that Mother had left her house keys in her other sweater pocket—the sweater which was in the front hall closet! We tried to remedy the situation, but we could not break into our own home! Using the neighbor's phone, my dad called a locksmith who opened our door. We . . . were . . . home, and believe me I hope nobody mentions the word "picnic" to me for a long, long time.

Lori Clark
Grade 7

Families

F - Fantastic
A - Absolutely Great
M - Magnificent
I - Incredible
L - Lovely
I - Ideal
E - Excellent
S - Superb

Craig Candler
Grade 4

My Mom

My mom is very special to me. She buys me everything. When I am sick she takes care of me—and even when I am not sick. My mom is a hard worker. She works at home and at her job. My mom is also my best friend. I can talk to her when I am happy. I am so glad she is my mom.

Erene Velakis
Age 8

I like to do my writing mostly at school. I like to write about my friends.

Erene Velakis

MOM

Always been there...

Always been there
Always cared.
Always helped
Always shared.
Never cruel
Always fair.

Always good...Always there.

THANK YOU MOM.

Joseph Victor Rossi
Age 12

I always see my dad do things, and he's really fun.

Jeffery Ong

My Dad

My Dad is nice.
My Dad is gentle.
My Dad cares for people.
He likes the family,
He's never mad.
He's smart and never quits.
He seems to know what to do
And he's the best!

Jeffery Ong
Age 9

MEET DANITRA BROWN

by Nikki Grimes
Illustrated by Floyd Cooper

YOU OUGHTA MEET DANITRA BROWN

You oughta meet Danitra Brown,
the most splendiferous girl in town.
I oughta know, 'cause she's my friend.

She's not afraid to take a dare.
If something's hard, she doesn't care.
She'll try her best, no matter what.

She doesn't mind what people say.
She always does things her own way.
Her spirit's old, my mom once said.

I only know I like her best
'cause she sticks out from all the rest.
She's only she—Danitra Brown.

MOM AND ME ONLY

Some kids at school have a mom and a dad.
I've got Mom and me only.
On Parents' Night it makes me mad
that it's Mom and me only.
"You've got it good," Danitra says when I am sad.
"Your mama loves you twice as much, is that so bad?"
Danitra knows just what to say to make me glad.
With her around, I'm never lonely.

CULTURE

Mom says I need culture, whatever that means;
then she irons some dumb dress, makes me take off my jeans,
drags me to the theatre for some stupid show.
(It turns out to be fun, but I don't let her know.)
Next day I tell Danitra what the play was about,
then we go to her bedroom and act it all out.
We play all of the parts, and pretend that we're stars
like the ones that step out of those long shiny cars.
Then Danitra starts dancing while I sing the main song,
and she promises that next time she'll come along.
We decide we like culture, whatever that means,
but we both think that culture goes better with jeans!

ABOUT THE AUTHOR NIKKI GRIMES

Nikki Grimes calls herself an artist rather than a writer. It's easy to see why — she's also interested in music, theatre, photography, and handicrafts. But when it comes to writing, poetry is what Nikki likes to write most of all. She has written many books for children, including a whole book of poems about Danitra, called *Meet Danitra Brown*.

Chrissy stepped from her tree house porch onto the wide board, reached for Leah's waiting hand, and walked across. She entered Leah's tree house and looked around.

There was no rug, and the only books were her own that Leah had borrowed. But there was a bowl of fruit, a wastebasket, and curtains at the windows. The walls were covered with portraits of beautiful women — the most beautiful women Chrissy had ever seen.

"I like your art collection, Leah," Chrissy said.

"They're left over from where my mom works," Leah explained. "She works at a beauty parlor, and they get pictures of all the new hairstyles. These are last year's."

"You can't tell. They look brand new."

"My house isn't as nice as yours," Leah added. "I said it was better inside, but it isn't, really."

"I don't really have carpeting," Chrissy admitted. "Only an old rug. And I don't have curtains, or a single picture on my walls."

"I could let you have one of my pictures. Two, even. You can have the blonde shag and the auburn blunt cut."

"My grandpa had paint left over. He could paint the outside of your house so we'd match. But I'm afraid we don't have another doorbell."

"Now that my sign says WELCOME, I don't think I need a doorbell," Leah said.

"I don't really hate you, Leah," Chrissy said.

"I don't really hate you, either," Leah replied.

They sat together on Leah's porch and looked around happily.

"What do you think is the best part of a tree house, Chrissy?" Leah asked.

Chrissy thought. She looked over at her own house, with its shutters and brass hinges. She looked around at Leah's, with its bowl of bright apples and its yellow curtains.

"The *very* best part," she said finally, "is the bridge."

ABOUT THE AUTHOR LOIS LOWRY

Lois Lowry has written over twenty books for young people, including the Newbery Award-winning *Number the Stars*. She feels that she is successful as a writer when her books help young people "answer their own questions about life, identity, and human relationships."

"I like all sorts of people, the ocean, sailboats, music and movies," says Lois. "Most of all I like the excitement I still feel, as I did when I was not quite four, when words go together to make sentences, and the sentences become stories."

Getting Along
A How-To Manual

by Catherine Rondina
Illustrated by Danielle Jones

Q: What's sometimes hot and sometimes not,
and something you need every day?
A: A stove. *Or* a friendship!

Have you ever thought how operating a stove is like making a friendship work? Probably not. Let's pretend, though, that your friendship is like the stove in your kitchen. Your stove has dials that show different settings and temperatures. That's a bit like all the different types of friendships you have with different people. Some friendships stay cool, and others are warm. Some are super-hot!

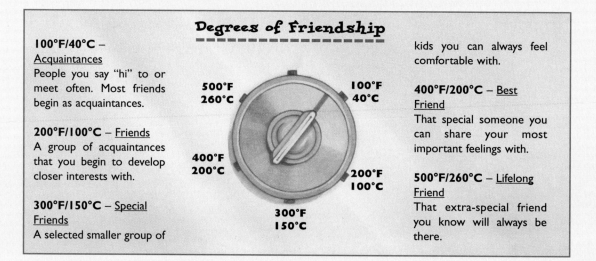

Degrees of Friendship

100°F/40°C –
<u>Acquaintances</u>
People you say "hi" to or meet often. Most friends begin as acquaintances.

200°F/100°C – <u>Friends</u>
A group of acquaintances that you begin to develop closer interests with.

300°F/150°C – <u>Special Friends</u>
A selected smaller group of kids you can always feel comfortable with.

400°F/200°C – <u>Best Friend</u>
That special someone you can share your most important feelings with.

500°F/260°C – <u>Lifelong Friend</u>
That extra-special friend you know will always be there.

Sometimes it's hard to know how to make stoves and friendships work. Stoves come with manuals, or how-to booklets, to help with that problem. This is a manual to help you understand and operate your friendships better.

Table of Contents

Important Instructions: *Getting Along: A How-To Manual*
is divided into four main sections.

Section 1
Installation and Assembly
(Putting a Friendship Together)

Everybody needs friends. The problem is, you need to know what to look for in a friend. Here are some of the parts you should try to put together when building a friendship.

- A friend often shares your interests and values.
- Friends should respect each other's feelings and differences.
- A true friend knows how you feel about certain things without having to be told.
- Friends should trust each other—good friends never hurt each other on purpose.
- A friend understands that both of you can make mistakes. When you do make a mistake, it's important to say you're sorry.

Being Your Own Friend First

The first step in being a good friend is to think about the kind of person you are. Try writing down the answers to some of the following questions:

- What things do you like about yourself? What things could you improve on? Remember, you can like yourself and still admit you're not perfect!
- What do you like to do best? least?
- Which of your interests would you like a friend to share?
- Why would you be a good friend for someone to have?

Operating Instructions
(Do's and Don'ts of Friendship)

How do you make a friendship work? Here are some points you may want to consider.

- Do listen. Listening shows you have respect for your friend's opinions.
- Don't talk behind your friend's back. Doing that hurts your friend and it hurts you, too. It shows everyone that you can't be trusted.
- Do keep secrets. However, if the secret is something really serious, you should ask the advice of a parent or of another adult you can trust.
- Do be considerate. Decide how your friend would feel before you do or say something that might be hurtful. Be sure to show appreciation when a friend does something nice.
- Don't take a friend for granted. Teasing and insults can destroy trust in a friendship.

Try to be the kind of friend you'd want to have.

Problem Solving and Service
(Talking Out Your Troubles)

Even good stoves malfunction sometimes. That means they don't work right. Friendships are the same—even the best of friends have their ups and downs. Here are some steps to follow to help you solve conflict in your friendships.

 1. **Stop**. The first step in problem solving is to stop and think. Stay calm and think over the problem to yourself.

2. **Identify**. The next step is to decide why you or your friend are upset, or why you have a problem.

3. **Think.** Brainstorm ways to solve the problem. Even if your ideas seem a bit silly, a good laugh might lighten up the situation.

4. **Agree.** Next, try to agree on a way to solve the problem. What solution makes the most sense and is fair to both of you?

5. **Plan.** The last step is planning how to make the idea you agreed on work. Talk about the steps you need to take to make the solution work. Once you've begun talking, you're already on your way to solving your problems.

What should you do if you can't solve your problem after trying these steps? One good idea is to bring in a mediator. That's a person who's not involved in the problem, and who can listen to both sides and try to help. A mediator could be another friend, or a sister or brother, or an adult you and your friend both trust.

Long-Term Care
(Keeping Long-Distance Friendships)

Keeping a friendship going for a long time isn't always easy. For instance, things may change in your life. You or your friend might move away, or one of you might have to change schools. This doesn't mean you have to stop being friends, though.

The main thing is to keep in touch. If you still live near each other, you can visit. If not, try writing to each other to keep your friendship going. There are lots of ways you can do this, such as writing letters, becoming computer keypals, or joining the same computer networks or interest groups .

Here are some tips on being a good long-distance pal:

- Write letters or send audio tapes often. Remember, it's always fun to get mail.
- Talk about what's going on in your neighborhood, and ask about your friend's neighborhood.

- Send pictures of your favorite musicians, actors, or sports stars. Photos or videotapes of yourself and your family and your pets are fun too.
- Tell jokes or funny stories about things that have happened.

Warranty

If you look at a stove manual, you'll find it always includes a warranty. That's a guarantee or promise that the stove will work properly for a certain number of years. Unfortunately, there's no warranty on a friendship. That's because friendships are more complicated than stoves, and take a lot more skills to operate. As you know by now, the best way to make sure your friendships last is to work at them. To make and keep a friend, you have to be a friend.

We hope you enjoyed reading this manual, and that you'll find it useful.

Who's Scared?

by Alison Lohans

Illustrated by Luc Melanson

S am hurried along the side of the creek, not stopping to watch the families of ducks or run a stick through the cat-tails as he usually did.

On the other side of the creek was Ryan Brady, the neighborhood bully, kicking up clods of dirt.

Sam looked away and walked faster. He was afraid of Ryan, who was a year older and quite a bit bigger. Sometimes Ryan took things from smaller kids, and once in a while he beat somebody up. Sam draped his windbreaker over his shoulder, hoping Ryan wouldn't notice the bulges in his back pockets. In one was Sam's baseball card collection. In the other, carefully wrapped in Saran, were three of Mrs. Wilson's wonderful chocolate chip cookies.

Ryan's presence wasn't the only reason to hurry. The Blue Jays were playing later on, and Sam wanted to get home to watch the game on TV. Besides, ominous storm clouds were rolling in. Prairie thunderstorms could blow in awfully quickly, and Sam knew he probably wouldn't make it home without getting wet. Just then thunder growled, not too far away.

"I bet you're scared of thunder!" Ryan yelled across the water.

"Who's scared?" Sam shouted back, more afraid of Ryan than the storm. He wanted to add that thunder never hurt anyone, only lightning could, but his heart lurched at the thought of a confrontation with the bigger boy.

Large drops of rain splatted into the dust at his feet. Sam ran. Mom might fuss at him for staying out in the storm. If that happened, he wouldn't have time to sneak up to his room before the game to eat his cookies. He'd have to share them with his little sister Danielle.

"Scaredy cat!"

Sam glanced across the water as Ryan yelled. "I am not! I'm just—" But he didn't want to have to explain. If he did, he'd never make it home with his cookies, let alone his baseball cards.

"Sure, sure, scaredy cat!" Ryan started running too.

What was Ryan trying to do, corner him so he could pick on him? The wooden footbridge spanning the creek wasn't far away, and Ryan could be across it in no time.

FLASH! BOOM!

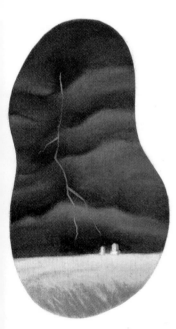

The storm was nearly overhead, the dark clouds seething in a scalloped pattern that Dad said sometimes came before a twister. And suddenly the rain was sluicing down so hard that Sam had to keep wiping it out of his face just to see. Ryan or no Ryan, he'd have to find cover quickly. It was dangerous to stay out in the open during a thunderstorm. Besides, hail might be on its way, and he didn't feel like getting a faceful of stinging ice pellets.

The footbridge was the closest safe place. Sam made a run for it and crouched beneath the strong boards.

Lightning spilled over everything in a pale flash. Thunder rumbled like a dinosaur burping. But through the noise Sam heard quick footsteps thudding on the wooden planks directly above him. He wrapped his arms tighter around his legs and hunched his shoulders up. Maybe Ryan would run on by in a mad dash to get home.

But in the next instant he had company. "Scaredy cat! Chicken liver scaredy cat!" Ryan taunted.

Sam shrank backward. His mouth opened, but no words

came out. In the dim eerie light cast by the storm clouds, deepened by the shadow of the footbridge, Ryan's face looked larger and paler than usual, and his freckles stood out almost like a sprinkling of chicken pox. Sam looked fearfully at Ryan's hands. At any minute they might reach out to poke him, grab him, or maybe push him into the water. But for the time being they were clenched so tightly around something that his knuckles looked white.

CRACK! It was the unmistakable sound of lightning hitting something nearby, maybe a tree, maybe a power pole. Sam gasped, but deafening thunder drowned him out. Next to him Ryan seemed to quiver for an instant, but right away he straightened up and nearly banged his head on the boards overhead.

"Hope it hit the school," he said sullenly in the lull after the thunder.

"Couldn't have been the school," Sam said. "It was too close." He peered out into the storm, wondering whether he should make a run for it. But in the next moment, pea-sized hailstones were clattering down, littering everything with white.

"Think you know it all, huh? Well, I'm telling you, you're just a baby." Ryan's jeering almost made the prospect of running through hail seem inviting.

Sam took a deep breath. "I am not."

"Oh sure, sure, little baby scared of a storm." For a minute neither boy spoke. Then Ryan looked down and unclenched his hands. Disgust flashed across his face. "RATBARF!" he yelled, and flung pieces of something Sam couldn't recognize into the water. Then he sat back and stared at the hail. Sam noticed that he definitely shuddered at the next roar of thunder.

Was *Ryan* scared of the storm? Why else would he bother

crouching under the bridge with a smaller kid? Pleasant surprise wiggled through Sam, and suddenly the bigger boy didn't seem quite so scary.

"What did you throw away?" he asked after a pause.

"None of your business." Ryan's hands dangled loosely in front of his knees. It looked as if crumbs were sticking to them.

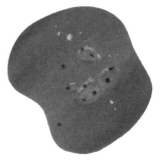

Cookie crumbs! Cautiously Sam's hand crept back to check his pockets. His own cookies were still intact, his baseball cards still there. Why would old Ryan get so upset over a couple of smushed wet cookies?

BOOM!

Ryan jumped. Now Sam was sure. The bully was afraid. Pleased with his discovery, Sam couldn't help rubbing it in. "I bet it was cookies you threw away," he said. "Chocolate chip cookies from Mrs. Wilson." After all, Mrs. Wilson gave cookies to half the kids in the neighborhood, even to Ryan if he went to the trouble of being polite.

"What do you care?" Ryan muttered.

Sam just smiled. The hail was abating and the storm was passing on. He could tell by using a special trick Dad had taught him. He could get home safely now without worrying about being hit by lightning. Even better, he could leave old bully Brady shivering under the footbridge, scared stiff. It wasn't often a guy caught Brady in a tight spot.

The hail stopped. Only rain spattered down. Sam stepped out into it, putting on his windbreaker. FLASH! Slowly he began to count. One hippopotamus, two hippopotamus, three hippopotamus . . . The thunder didn't roar until he'd reached six hippopotamus. That meant the lightning was well over a kilometre and a half away.

"Where are you going, chicken?" Ryan yelled. "Betcha get hit by lightning."

"Not a chance," Sam said confidently. For a moment he wondered whether he should give Ryan one of his cookies— not that he deserved any. But Ryan was a bigger kid, and if a

little guy offered him a cookie for no good reason, it might just look like that little kid felt sorry for old Ryan Brady. That would never do. Ryan Brady might decide to make things extra tough for the smaller guy.

"Betcha get hit—you'll sizzle like bacon." Ryan made oinking sounds.

"No way," Sam called back casually over his shoulder. He felt like running, but he made sure his feet kept to a slow walk over the slippery clay. He didn't want to take any chances of spoiling his classy exit by falling in front of Ryan.

FLASH! One hippopotamus, two hippopotamus . . . Sam looked back one more time. Ryan was still huddled under the bridge, peering out at him. He looked miserable and scared, but even more satisfying, he was losing face—watching a little guy walk away into a storm. Nine hippopotamus . . . BOOM!

"Hey!" Sam yelled. "I know a special trick to tell how far away the lightning is. Remind me to tell you about it sometime."

"How?" Ryan yelled back.

"Haven't got time now," Sam replied, still walking. "I want

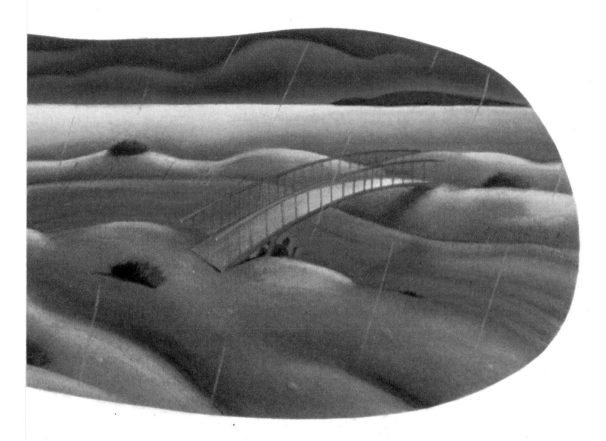

to catch the beginning of the baseball game. It's Blue Jays vs. Oakland A's." With luck, Ryan would want to see the game too—and he had to turn down a different street to get home.

He'd still have to face Mom and change his wet clothes before he got near the TV. He might even have to give Danielle one of his cookies. But what was one cookie, compared to what had just happened? Getting the best of big bully Brady was going to feel good for an awfully long time.

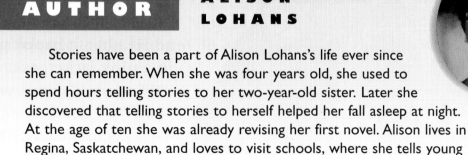

ABOUT THE AUTHOR

ALISON LOHANS

Stories have been a part of Alison Lohans's life ever since she can remember. When she was four years old, she used to spend hours telling stories to her two-year-old sister. Later she discovered that telling stories to herself helped her fall asleep at night. At the age of ten she was already revising her first novel. Alison lives in Regina, Saskatchewan, and loves to visit schools, where she tells young authors to "get characters in trouble, and the story grows out of that."

Zeena nodded, too disappointed to speak. She found a place by a window on the wide back seat with some boys.

The driver, Gwen's father, closed the door. Scarcely had the bus started through the suburbs toward Pike Lake when the boys began scuffling. Brent Dallen accidentally kicked Zeena with his heavy hiking boot. He sat up straight, looking at her with a funny expression as he mumbled, "Sorry, Zebreena."

His politeness hurt. Boys weren't usually formal except with strangers. They called their friends by nicknames—Slim, Fats, and the shortest person in the group they called Stretch. They always called her Zebreena.

Her eyes grew moist as she stared across the frozen land. Back home, in the part of B.C. where she'd lived, there were no lakes close by, no skating rinks, so she'd learned to ski and snowshoe. But once she'd mentioned snowshoeing, Gwen had said, "Sounds kinda dumb to me." So Zeena's father had bought her skates, but she could not take even three steps without falling flat on her face.

As the bus crossed the highway, she debated to herself whether to get out at her stop. The thought that Heather might be disappointed made her hesitate. But Heather was whispering and giggling with Betty Ann and Gwen and had probably forgotten her. She waited too long and through the whirling flurries she saw her home fade into the whiteness. Farther on, she knew the snow was falling more heavily when she could barely see Heather's house.

Beyond the Robertson farm, the road curved and turned through the deepening snow. Halfway around Devil's Curve, the driver shifted to low as the bus entered a drift. Zeena pretended great interest in the snow-burdened willow bushes they passed, as she secretly wished she'd left the bus when they had reached the road leading to her home.

After the slow progress, they speeded up as they rolled across the stretch of parkland, coming at last to a small school that seemed to huddle down, protecting itself from blustering wind. It faced a small pond which the boys were clearing of snow with long-handled scoops. Beyond the hills of snow they were forming were rows of wooden benches.

A tall slim teacher with a berry-red nose walked up to the bus. "I'm Mrs. Weller. Welcome to you all and may the best team win."

Gwen's father answered, "Booker is my name and I'm in charge of this motley crew. Where can they change?"

"There in the basement, and we'd better start right away, Mr. Booker. The way it's snowing, we'll have very little time. Who's your captain?"

Brent Dallen stretched out his hand. A tall boy with a good-natured face, he wore his school-colored jacket with a jaunty air.

"I'm captain, Mrs. Weller. We'll be ready in a sec."

"Fine. Then I'll have our boys put up the flags for the relay race."

There was an air of excitement among the students of both schools. Many of the Cloverdale girls and boys went over to examine the silver cup that was on display. Donated by Miss Holliston years before to promote winter sports, it had been won twice by each school. All were keenly aware that today would decide which school would win permanent possession of the trophy.

Zebreena took her place at the end of the bench, and she had to put her foot out to keep from falling off when the girls crowded beside her. Gwen saw the movement and said, "Sorry, Zebreena." She didn't sound very concerned; neither did she move to make more space.

After that, Zeena didn't feel as if it were her school competing. She felt like an outsider. The only times she really felt a stir of interest were when Brent won the figure skating event, and later when Heather was entered in the relay race. Slim was ahead in the first lap when he handed the stick to Heather. Skating as never before, she finished in a dead heat with her boy opponent, handing the stick to Buzz. He slipped as he started off, and barely crossed the finish line ahead of his opposition.

The Cloverdale students nearly went wild, for they needed the points of the relay race to win the trophy. Mrs. Weller smiled as she handed the cup to Brent, and the students, yelling and laughing, snake-danced behind him to the bus.

Mr. Booker was a good driver, and they had no trouble through the blinding snowfall until they reached Devil's Curve. Suddenly, there was a skid, a lurch. "Hold on, everybody. We're slipping." Mr. Booker's voice was strained.

The wheels of the bus slewed sideways as, in slow motion, the bus skidded, tipped, then righted itself to come to a stop in the snow-filled ditch.

"We're stuck," Brent gasped.

Mr. Booker started forward in low, then backward, trying to rock the vehicle out of the heavily packed snow. He gained a few more metres, but each attempt only packed the wheels more tightly. They were trapped.

"Could we back up to Heather's house?"

"Far too many turns! I'd be sure to go off the road even if I could get back onto it."

Betty Ann giggled nervously. "Do we have to stay on the bus all night?"

"I certainly hope not!" Mr. Booker answered. His voice sounded worried, even more worried than he would let on. "We have enough gas to reach the Robertsons' but the tank will be empty before morning if I keep the motor running to have the heater going. And without the heater we'd freeze." Zeena noticed that he didn't add, "to death."

The sudden silence warned him that he had frightened them, and he added more cheerfully, "I'll have to go for the tow truck. I won't be long."

Mr. Booker told them to keep the door closed, but most of them stepped outside to watch him start back along the road.

He plunged through the drifts, sometimes up to his knees in the snow. He hadn't gone far when he fell and they heard a low moan.

After a few minutes Mr. Booker crawled slowly back, almost hidden beneath a covering of white. The boys ran to help him. "I've twisted my ankle, I can't go on."

After helping him into the bus, Brent cut the man's boot and they saw that his ankle was discolored and badly swollen.

"We're in real trouble!" Brent said.

Zebreena picked up the knife Brent had dropped and plunged through the snow to the nearest red willow bush. It was partly buried, but she found some branches she felt were suitable. After she collected enough for her purpose she carried them back to the bus.

No one paid any attention to what she was doing until she picked up Mr. Booker's boot, removed the leather lacing, and after bending one of the willow whips, tied the ends together in an oval loop.

"What are you making?" Brent asked her.

"A snowshoe," Zeena said. "It won't sink into the snow, so you can walk on the top."

"Great idea! Why didn't I think of that!" Brent said. Eagerly he reached out to Slim's boots, "Let me have your leather laces. You too, Toad."

With Brent and Heather helping, Zebreena made a second loop, and by weaving a cross-web of leather thongs, she soon had a crude but practical pair of snowshoes.

Zeena showed Brent how to fasten the lashings to his boots. He started out with enthusiasm, but Zeena realized in a moment that it was his first time on snowshoes. He scooped up snow on the rounded ends and after six steps he stumbled and fell forward into a drift. Grinning sheepishly, he dusted himself off and tried again, only to go sprawling once more. After his fourth fall, Mr. Booker called to him, "Enough! Enough! Brent! You'll break your neck."

"And it seemed like such a good idea," agreed Gwen. All of a sudden her eyes brightened and she turned to Zebreena.

"Do you know how to snowshoe?"

Zeena nodded. "I've been doing it for years," she admitted.

"I don't like sending a girl," Mr. Booker said. His voice sounded worried.

"I'll be all right," Zeena assured him, now quite confident. "That is, if the boys can spare a couple of extra laces, in case any break on the way."

Brent gave her his laces and tied on her snowshoes. She started forward, lifting the toes slightly to avoid scooping up snow, moving with a brisk jogging step that carried her lightly over the snow. She used two spare whips for balance.

"Look at her go!" Brent cried in astonishment. "She just zips along!"

Beyond the stranded bus the going was easier. Zebreena plodded doggedly on, breath steaming before her pink face. A wave of weariness overtook her but she stopped only for a short rest and to tuck her red scarf more securely about her ears. She was still a kilometre from the Robertson farm. From then on it was a fight against fatigue, her feet growing heavier with each step.

At last, almost exhausted, she reached the Robertson house. Heather's mother, a sweet-faced woman, opened the door. "Come

inside the porch out of the cold," Mrs. Robertson said. Teeth chattering, Zebreena explained what had happened.

"Let me help you off with your wet things. I'll phone the city garage to send out a tow truck."

Mr. Robertson removed her snowshoes, took her coat, and led her into the warm kitchen while Heather's mother phoned.

"The tow truck will start out immediately," she said a minute later. "I called your mother and I'll phone the other parents." She turned to her husband, "John, will you fix a hot bowl of soup for this young girl?"

A bowl of vegetable soup and three cups of hot chocolate later, Zeena's eyes grew heavy. She gladly accepted Mrs. Robertson's

invitation to lie on the chesterfield in front of a crackling fire. Zebreena slept.

It seemed as if she'd hardly closed her eyes before she was wakened by shouts and laughter. Girls and boys were trooping into the house. Mr. Booker limped in with the help of the tow truck man. They were all safe.

Heather ran around the chesterfield and hugged Zebreena. "You saved us from a miserable night, Zebreena. Maybe from even freezing to death." She paused, smiling. "Thank goodness you were so quick."

"Quick as a zipper!" Brent grinned.

"Of course. Our Zipper is even quicker!" Heather declared. "Teach me to use the snowshoes, Zip?"

"I'd be glad to," Zebreena said happily. "Teach me to skate?"

"Sure thing."

"We all will," said Slim.

"That was a terribly long way for you to go—and all alone too," Gwen said. "Are you warm now, Zip?"

Zebreena's eyes brimmed at so much attention. "Oh, wonderfully warm, all through," she said. There was a slight catch in her voice.

That day the Cloverdale School won an important silver trophy, but Zebreena, now called Zipper, won much more—now she had a whole class of good friends.

ABOUT THE AUTHOR   MARY C. WOOD

Mary C. Wood started writing when her children brought home stories about characters who were just too perfect to be believable. When she became a grandmother she said that her grandchildren were her best critics. Mary lived in Saskatoon and collaborated on a series of children's mysteries that focus on historical sites on the western prairies.

78

Making New Friends Is Special

I make new friends by including them because they may be lonely. You should also be kind to new friends because they don't want a mean friend. Be trusting and don't lie. A good friend would listen to them and their problems. Being polite and using your manners will show that you are not rude. Being helpful is nice but cheating is not. You should be fair; being selfish is not nice. Be cheerful. If your friend is sad, it will make him or her feel better. That is how you make new friends.

Genny Hay

Age 8

I like writing short stories or poems. I like writing in my room at my desk because it is nice and quiet. Sometimes after I take a rest, my mind runs wild with ideas.

Genny Hay

I love writing stories but I like writing poems better. I get my ideas from my heart. I just sit down and concentrate. I can do my poems better in the class, but I can also do them at home

Nicole Vandenberk

Friendship

I never knew what friendship was until I met you.
Now I know what it is,
You're someone I can tell secrets to.
You are my best friend, you really care.
We do stuff together, we laugh and share.
I go to your house, you come to mine.
I have other friends but you're first in line.
If I ever lost you I would really cry.
I would cry so much I would almost die.
I hope you feel the same way for me.
Because you're the best friend there can ever be.

Nicole Vandenberk
Age 11

Student Writing

I'm a Hero!!!

It was my first day at hockey. I got number twelve. I met my coach. His name was Bob. Bob said that I'd be the goalie. I met a girl named Melissa. She took shots on me. I saved every one except for one. After that, Bob said to go and get the other goalie. Soon hockey was over. My mom picked me up.

"Mom," I said, "my coach's name is Bob and I have a new friend. Her name is Melissa. She took shots on me and I saved every one except for one."

We had supper early today. After supper, I went downstairs with my brother. He took shots on me. I saved every one. After that, Melissa phoned. She asked if we had a real game tomorrow. I said yes. I asked my dad if he ever played hockey.

He said, "Yes."

"Where did you play?"

"I played in Saskatoon for the Hawks."

"Was it fun?"

"Yes, it was."

Soon it was time for bed. All night I thought, "Who is going to win tomorrow?" I woke up in the morning at 8:00. It was a Saturday, so I didn't have to worry about school. I got dressed and went out into the kitchen. My mom was in there and had already made breakfast. I sat down at the table and ate. After that, I phoned Melissa. I said, "Almost all night I was thinking about who is going to win today."

"Me too," said Melissa.

I said, "Can you come over?"

"Just wait, I will see."

Soon Melissa was back and she could come over. "Come over as soon as you can."

"Okay, I'd better say goodbye then."

She was over in five minutes. She was out of breath. I said to her, "You were sure fast." We went downstairs and she took shots on me. I saved every one. After, when we got bored, I went and asked my mom if Melissa could stay for lunch and she said yes. For lunch we had sandwiches. Then we took Melissa home. When we came back, I had to get ready for hockey. After, my dad took me to hockey, and I went into the dressing room and sat by Melissa. Soon we had to get on the ice. We were playing against the Jets. They took shots on me and I saved them.

In a minute, Melissa scored a goal. The scoreboard was set at 1-0. Before long, the score was 5-4 for the Jets. There were only two minutes left and everyone on our team was disappointed. Melissa accidentally lost control of the puck right in front of me and I just about panicked! I got the puck and shot it as hard as I could. I couldn't believe it! I scored a goal! I was the hero!

NICOLE SPERLIE
Age 9